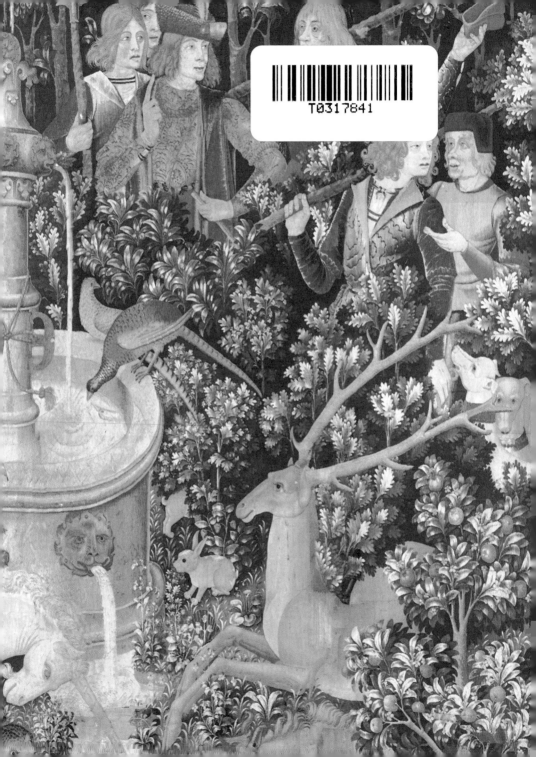

ODDITIES & CURIOSITIES

Sticker, Color & Activity Book

chartwell
books

Quarto

© 2024 Quarto Publishing Group USA Inc.

This edition published in 2024 by Chartwell Books,
an imprint of The Quarto Group
142 West 36th Street, 4th Floor
New York, NY 10018 USA
T (212) 779-4972 F (212) 779-6058
www.Quarto.com

Contains content originally published as *Handmade Lip Balm* (2018),
The Witch's Complete Guide to Crystals (2022), *Astrology: A Guided
Workbook* (2022), *Tarot: A Guided Workbook* (2022), and *Make Your
Own Resin Jewelry* (2023) by Chartwell Books, an imprint of The Quarto
Group, 142 West 36th Street, 4th Floor, New York, NY 10018 USA.

10 9 8 7 6 5 4 3 2 1

Chartwell titles are also available at discount for retail, wholesale,
promotional, and bulk purchase. For details, contact the Special Sales
Manager by email at specialsales@quarto.com or by mail at The Quarto
Group, Attn: Special Sales Manager, 100 Cummings Center Suite 265D,
Beverly, MA 01915, USA.

ISBN: 978-0-7858-4428-0

Publisher: Wendy Friedman
Senior Publishing Manager: Meredith Mennitt
Senior Design Manager: Michael Caputo
Editor: Jennifer Kushnier
Designer: Kate Sinclair

All stock photos and design elements ©Shutterstock

Printed in Shaoguan, China. SL0324.

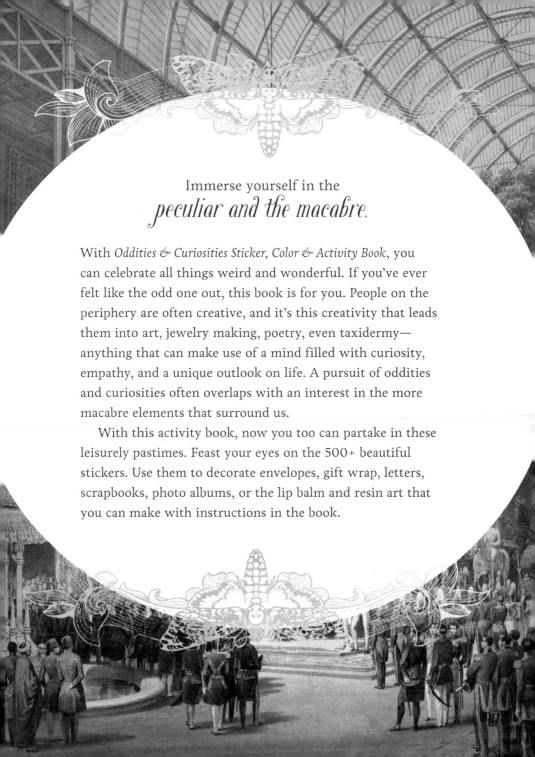

Immerse yourself in the
peculiar and the macabre.

With *Oddities & Curiosities Sticker, Color & Activity Book*, you can celebrate all things weird and wonderful. If you've ever felt like the odd one out, this book is for you. People on the periphery are often creative, and it's this creativity that leads them into art, jewelry making, poetry, even taxidermy— anything that can make use of a mind filled with curiosity, empathy, and a unique outlook on life. A pursuit of oddities and curiosities often overlaps with an interest in the more macabre elements that surround us.

With this activity book, now you too can partake in these leisurely pastimes. Feast your eyes on the 500+ beautiful stickers. Use them to decorate envelopes, gift wrap, letters, scrapbooks, photo albums, or the lip balm and resin art that you can make with instructions in the book.

To further relax and add fun to your free time, flip through the more than 50 activity and coloring pages. There are a variety of puzzles, mazes, trivia, and fun activities like hangman, picture matching, creating a Gothic name, cleansing crystals, and reading tarot or skulls.

With so many pages to look at, so many things to do, and so much joy to be had in these pages, *Oddities & Curiosities Sticker, Color & Activity Book* is the perfect book to have on hand when a free moment strikes. Whether you're a sticker lover, scrapbooker, crafter, colorer, or artist, you're sure to find something unique in this peculiar treasure trove!

Phrenology, the Strange Pseudoscience

Phrenology, or "skull reading," was a practice by which a practitioner felt a person's head to determine aspects of their natural aptitudes, character, personality, and tendencies. The idea behind it was that certain abilities were linked to specific areas of the brain, which phrenologists thought was composed of muscle. And, like other muscles when exercised, it was thought that the bumps on the skull were the results of bigger brain muscles in those areas—and dimples were associated with depleted muscles, or deficits. The theory was developed by German physician Franz Joseph Gall in the late 1700s. He called it "organology," but it was his assistant, physician Johann Gaspar Spurzheim, who coined the term that we know today.

Based on what Gall observed by measuring the skulls of his classmates as well as people in hospitals, asylums, and prisons, he developed a system of 27 "faculties" that he associated with different areas of the head; Spurzheim subsequently added 10 more. These faculties were grouped into areas such as domestic, selfish, moral, intellectual, literary, and reasoning. Below are these faculties, as recounted in the 1857 book *The Illustrated Self-Instructor in Phrenology and Physiology* by "practical phrenologists" O. S. and L. N. Fowler, who added their own subsets:

1. **AMATIVENESS**
   Sexual and connubial love.

2. **PHILOPROGENITIVENESS**
   Parental love.

3. **ADHESIVENESS**
   Friendship—sociability.

A. **UNION FOR LIFE**
   Love of one only.

4. **INHABITIVENESS**
   Love of home.

5. **CONTINUITY**
   One thing at a time.

6. **COMBATIVENESS**
   Resistance—defence.

7. **DESTRUCTIVENESS**
   Executiveness—force.

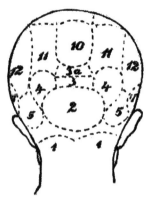
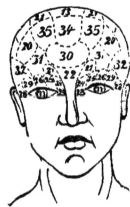

8. **ALIMENTIVENESS**
   Appetite, hunger.

9. **ACQUISITIVENESS**
   Accumulation.

10. **SECRETIVENESS**
    Policy—management.

11. **CAUTIOUSNESS**
    Prudence, provision.

12. **APPROBATIVENESS**
    Ambition—display.

13. **SELF-ESTEEM**
    Self-respect—dignity.

14. **FIRMNESS**
    Decision—perseverance.

15. **CONSCIENTIOUSNESS**
    Justice—equity.

16. **HOPE**
    Expectation—enterprise.

17. **SPIRITUALITY**
    Intuition—spiritual revery.

18. **VENERATION**
    Devotion—respect.

19. **BENEVOLENCE**
    Kindness—goodness.

20. **OBSTRUCTIVENESS**
    Mechanical ingenuity.

21. **IDEALITY**
    Refinement—taste—purity.

B. **SUBLIMITY**
   Love of grandeur.

22. **IMITATION**
    Copying—patterning.

23. **MINDFULNESS**
    Jocoseness—wit—fun.

24. **INDIVIDUALITY**
    Observation.

25. **FORM**
    Recollection of shape.

26. **SIZE**
    Measuring by the eye.

27. **WEIGHT**
    Balancing—climbing.

28. **COLOR**
    Judgment of colors.

29. **ORDER**
    Method—system—arrangement.

30. **CALCULATION**
    Mental arithmetic.

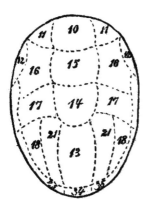
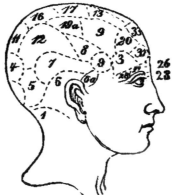

31. LOCALITY
Recollection of places.

32. EVENTUALITY
Memory of facts.

33. TIME
Cognizance of duration.

34. TUNE
Music—melody by ear.

35. LANGUAGE
Expression of ideas.

36. CAUSALITY
Applying causes to effects.

37. COMPARISON
Inductive reasoning.

C. HUMAN NATURE
Perception of motives.

D. AGREEABLENESS
Pleasantness—suavity.

Though discredited by the mid-19th century, phrenology has experienced bursts of popularity ever since. And though Gall and his followers were incorrect about the meaning of cranial hills and valleys, they were correct in ascribing parts of the brain to certain mental functions—something that sounds a lot like modern neuroscience. Phrenologists used a bust—something like a hard wig mannequin—to help map out a person's bumps and indentations, but by using the chart above, you can do the same with a friend. Gently run your fingers over the person's head, feeling for bumps and depressions, then compare the number from the chart to the previous list.

solution on page 161

solution on page 161

solution on page 162

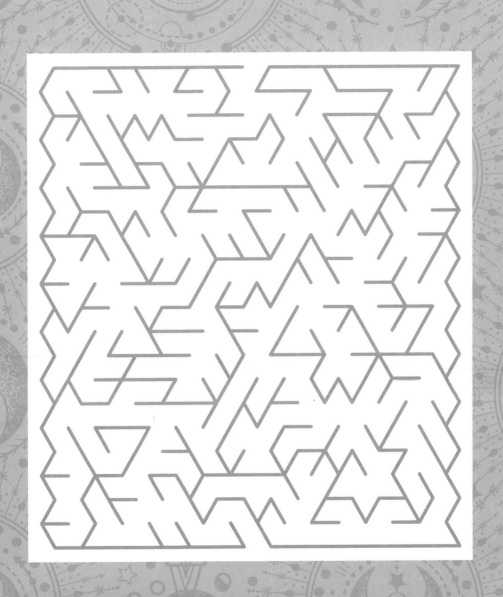

solution on page 162

solution on page 163

solution on page 163

solution on page 164

solution on page 164

solution on page 164

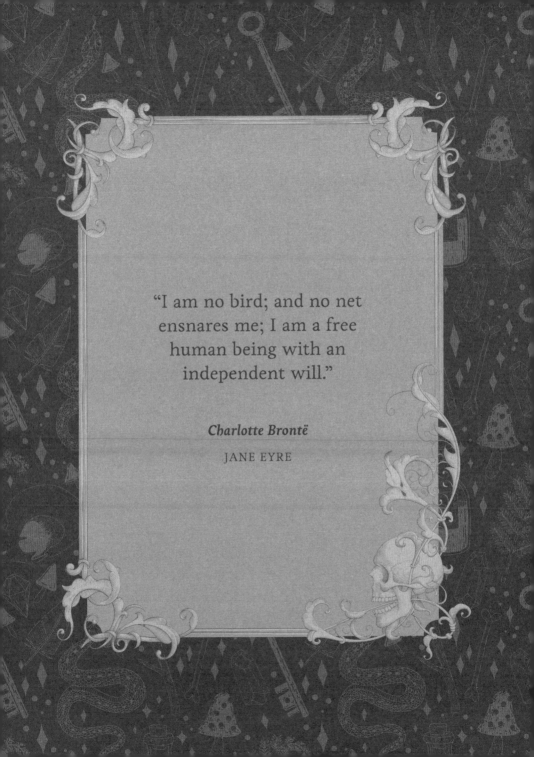

"I am no bird; and no net
ensnares me; I am a free
human being with an
independent will."

Charlotte Brontë

JANE EYRE

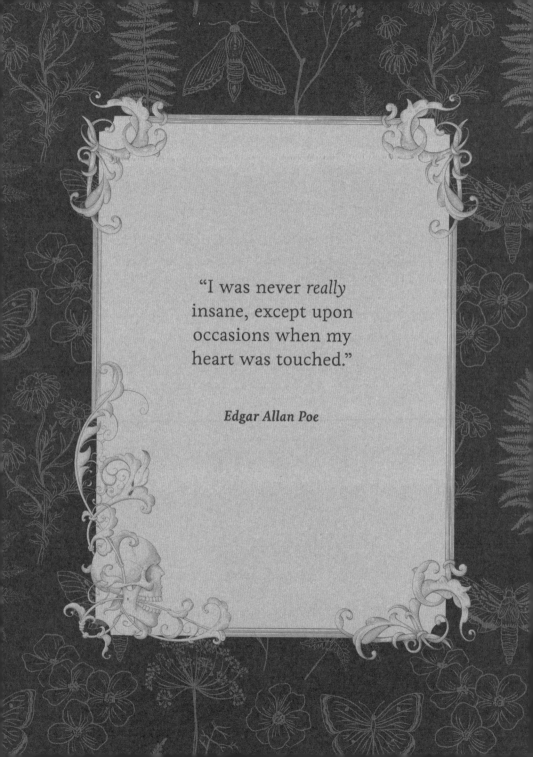

"I was never *really* insane, except upon occasions when my heart was touched."

Edgar Allan Poe

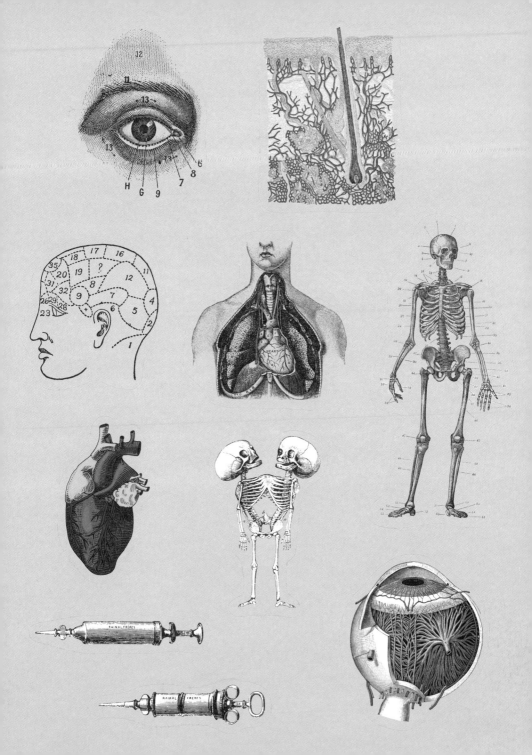

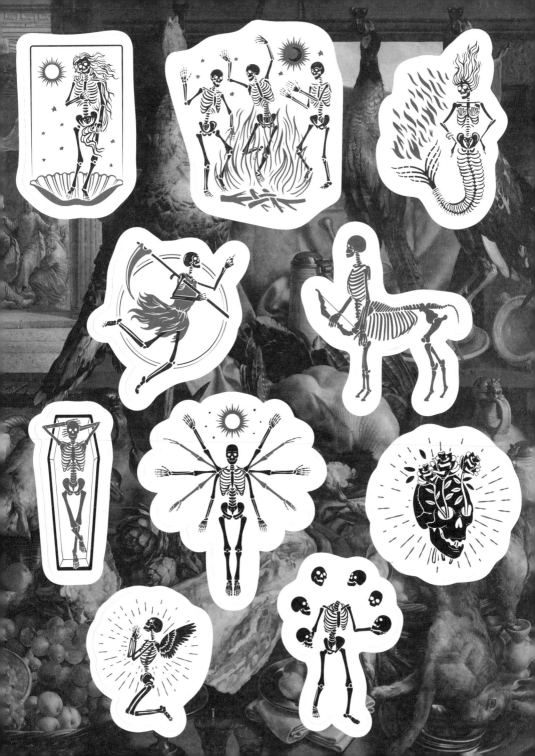

"There is no exquisite
beauty without some
strangeness in the
proportion."

Francis Bacon

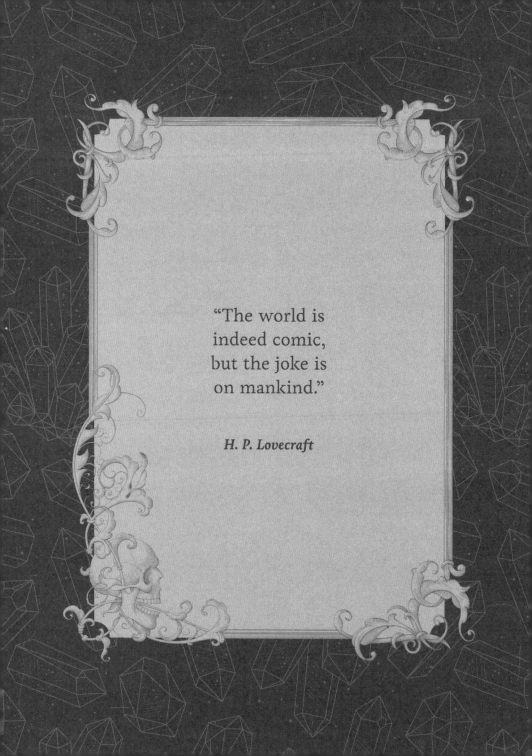

"The world is
indeed comic,
but the joke is
on mankind."

H. P. Lovecraft

Match the Beetle!

There are 30 types of beetles, making them the most common type of insect. See how many you can guess correctly.

Rhinoceros beetle

Ladybug

Atlas beetle

Caterpillar hunter

Tiger beetle

Deathwatch beetle

Weevil

Scarab beetle

Potato bug

Dung beetle

Stag beetle

Firefly

Whirligig

Hercules beetle

Sawyer beetle

Match the Beetle!
(answer key)

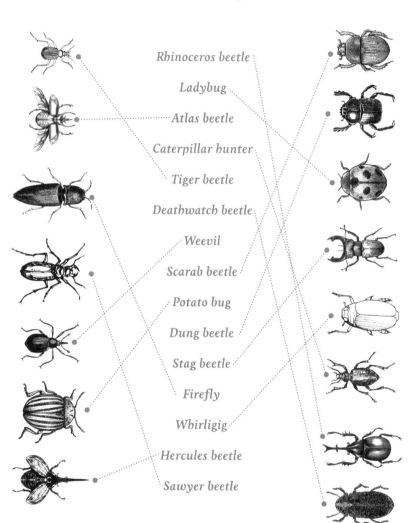

Rhinoceros beetle

Ladybug

Atlas beetle

Caterpillar hunter

Tiger beetle

Deathwatch beetle

Weevil

Scarab beetle

Potato bug

Dung beetle

Stag beetle

Firefly

Whirligig

Hercules beetle

Sawyer beetle

Match the Skull to the Animal!

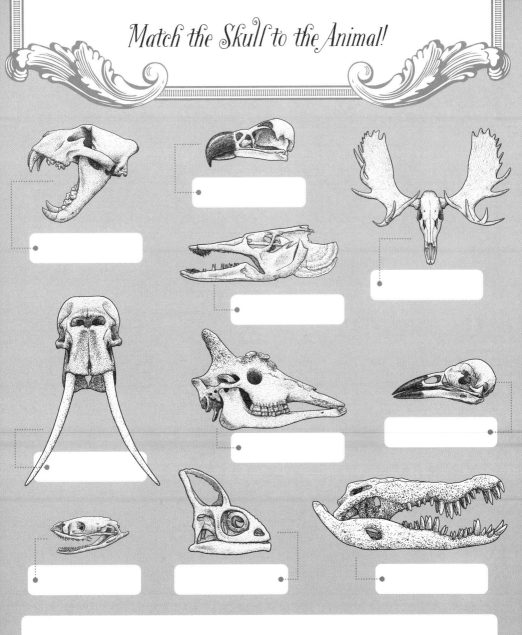

Moose	Giraffe	Pike	Elephant	Vulture
Crow	Chameleon	Lion	Adder	Crocodile

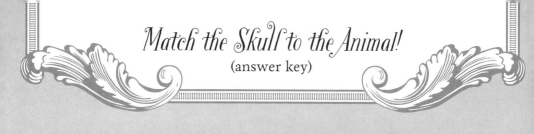

Match the Skull to the Animal!
(answer key)

Vulture

Lion

Pike

Moose

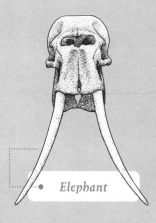

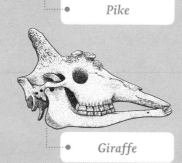

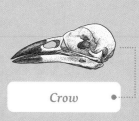

Giraffe

Crow

Elephant

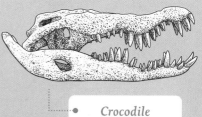

Adder

Chameleon

Crocodile

Crystal Energy

Crystals are naturally occurring materials with highly ordered atoms and a constant vibration. People throughout time have included crystals in their medicinal practices, religions, and ritual use. Crystal magic dates back centuries to when humans used the elements of nature for healing and other ritualistic purposes. Some crystal origins are tied back to ancient Egypt and India and are still prevalent in Native American culture.

The first written record of the use of minerals dates back to ancient Egypt. Minerals like galena and stilbite were crushed and used for make-up, especially around the eyes. Egyptians also used malachite—a copper-based mineral—to clean wounds due to their belief that it had an antimicrobial effect. Other civilizations saw the power of crystals as well. Babylonians used lapis lazuli to ward off evil, and the ancient Chinese used crystal healing as a form of medicine.

Over recent decades, a renewed interest in crystals has emerged, turning what was once an underground world into a highly accessible topic. Healers, shamans, energy workers, and many others continue to use crystals in their practices by connecting us with universal energy through crystals.

Crystals are often used in jewelry or in art, and knowing what their metaphysical properties are can enhance their appeal. On the following pages are some popular crystals and their meanings. What speaks to you?

AGATE *Grounding, Harmony, Confidence*

AMAZONITE
*Courage, Balance,
Communication*

AMBER *Courage, Psychic Shielding, Sensuality*

AMETHYST
*Wisdom, Intuition,
Calming*

ANGELITE *Divine Connection, Communication, Calming*

APATITE
*Communication,
Motivation,
Self-Acceptance*

APOPHYLLITE *Recovery, Vitality, Spirituality*

AQUAMARINE
*Happiness, Calming,
Inner Strength*

ARAGONITE *Creativity, Energy, Stability*

AVENTURINE
*Prosperity, Joy,
Abundance*

BISMUTH *Transformation, Focus, Courage*

**BLACK
MOONSTONE**
*Fertility, Protection,
Hope*

CARNELIAN
*Creativity,
Motivation,
Confidence*

CHALCEDONY Calming, Compassion, Balance

CHAROITE
*Intuition, Spiritual
Transformation, Divine
Guidance*

CHRYOPRASE Self Esteem, Confidence, Self-Love

CITRINE
*Confidence, Abundance,
Happiness*

COPPER Grounding, Desire, Energy Conduit

DIAMOND Fearlessness, Fortitude, Inner Power

DANBURITE
*Harmony, Happiness,
Calming*

DIOPTASE
*Love, Forgiveness,
Compassion*

DUMORTIERITE Harmony, Peace, Intuition

EMERALD
*Success, Wisdom,
Love*

EPIDOTE Spiritual Growth, Dream Enhancement, Healing

FLUORITE Focus, Decision Making, Insight

FUCHSITE
*Healing, Balance,
Detoxification*

GALENA Compassion, Love, Harmony

GARNET
*Revitalizing,
Passion, Devotion*

HEMATITE Grounding, Protection, Balance

HOWLITE
*Calming,
Purity, Cleansing*

JADE Good Luck, Prosperity, Positivity

KUNZITE
*Compassion,
Self Love, Well Being*

KYANITE Balance, Relaxation, Wisdom

LAPIS LAZULI Communication, Honesty, Wisdom

LABRADORITE
*Transformation,
Reflection, Loyalty*

LEPIDOLITE
*Uplifting, Calming,
Awareness*

MALACHITE
*Empathy,
Growth, Love*

MOONSTONE *Fertility, Intuition, Spiritual Purity*

MOOKAITE
*Strength, Courage,
Vitality*

OBSIDIAN *Protection, Grounding, Shielding*

ONYX *Willpower,
Focus, Protection*

OPAL *Memory Retention, Purity, Faith*

PERIDOT
*Vitality, Strength,
Abundance*

PIETERSITE *Personal Power, Self-Discovery, Energy*

PREHNITE
*Unconditional Love,
Precognition,
Angelic Connection*

PYRITE *Confidence, Protection, Abundance*

QUARTZ, CLEAR
*Clarity, Purify,
Cleanse*

QUARTZ, ROSE *Compassion, Empathy*

RHODONITE Love, Self-Worth, Wellbeing

RHODOCHROSITE
*Calming,
Love, Passion*

RUBY Concentration, Fearlessness, Passion

SELENITE Clarity, Positivity, Purification

SAPPHIRE
*Concentration,
Abundance, Wisdom*

SHUNGITE
*Grounding, EMF
Shielding, Purifying*

SODALITE Communication, Harmony, Self-Trust

SUNSTONE
*Uplifting, Positivity,
Confidence*

TIGER'S EYE Confidence, Courage, Fortune

TURQUOISE Expression, Inspiration, Tranquility

TOPAZ
*Self Realization,
Peace, Calming*

UNAKITE
*Balance,
Grounding, Vision*

Cleansing the Crystals

Anytime you get a new crystal—and especially if you're going to use it on artwork that you gift others—you will want to cleanse it to remove any negative energy. Smoke cleansing is the most common form of cleansing crystals. This method is safe for all of your gems. You can use a few different things to create smoke. Dried herbs and flowers like sage and lavender, incense, or resin all work very well. You will also need a fireproof dish and matches or a lighter.

Set fire to your smoke source and let the flame die down to a smolder; this should produce a steady stream of smoke. Be sure to hold it over the fireproof dish to catch rogue embers. One by one, move your crystals into the smoke, allowing it to wash over the entire stone. Envision the old energy being drawn out of the stone until it shines brightly.

Once you have cleansed all your crystals, place the incense, herb bundle, or resin in the fireproof dish, and keep it there until the smolder is out and it is safe to put away.

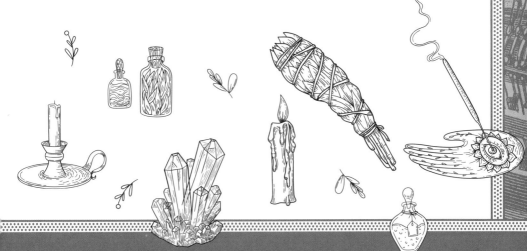

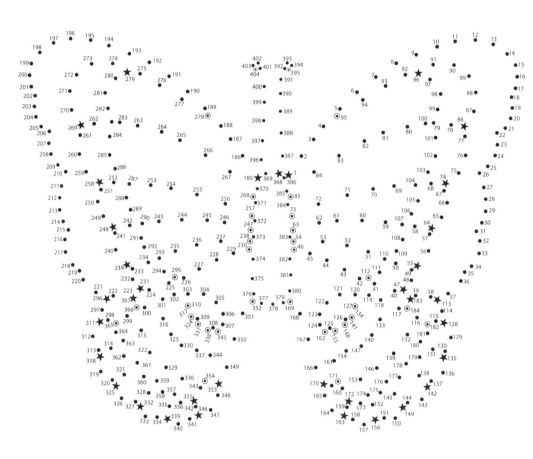

solution on page 166

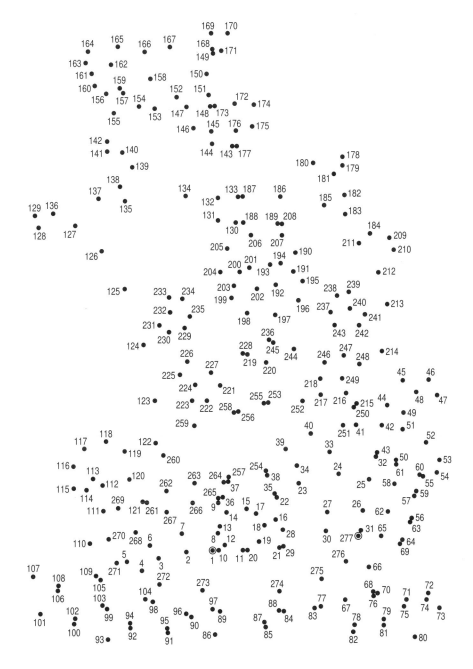

solution on page 167

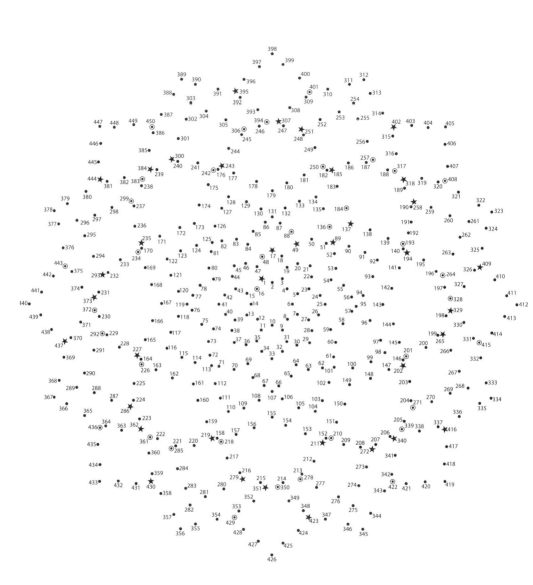

solution on page 168

solution on page 169

Trivia: Part I

1. What is considered the first gothic novel?

_____

2. Who wrote *The Turn of the Screw*?

_____

3. What was special about Dorian Gray's picture?

_____

4. True or False: Dr. Jekyll turned into Mr. Hyde when he drank wine.

_____

5. What character is this?

_____

6. True or False: Jane Austen wrote a parody of a gothic novel.

_____

7. Though Edgar Allen Poe is buried in Baltimore, in which city is his National Historic Site?

_____

8. What is the name of the English estate purchased by Dracula?

_____

9. *The Addams Family* characters started as a cartoon in which magazine?

_____

10. Which building in Washington, D.C., has a Darth Vader grotesque (gargoyle)?

_____

answers on page 165

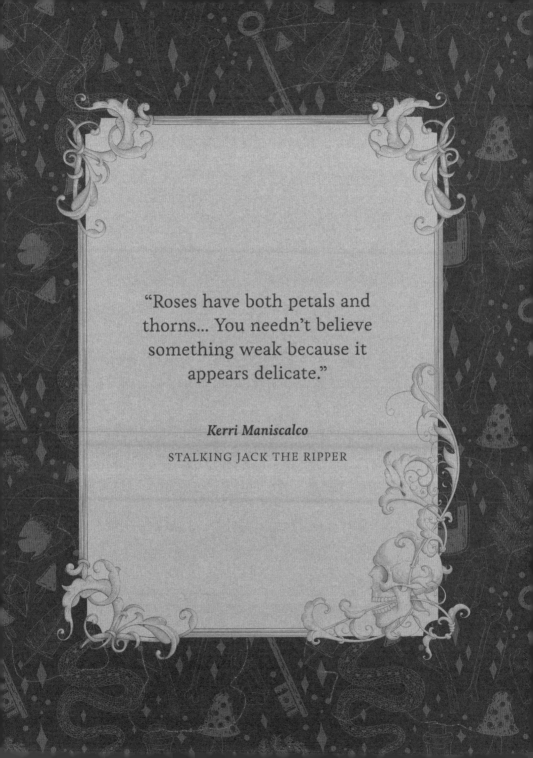

"Roses have both petals and thorns... You needn't believe something weak because it appears delicate."

Kerri Maniscalco

STALKING JACK THE RIPPER

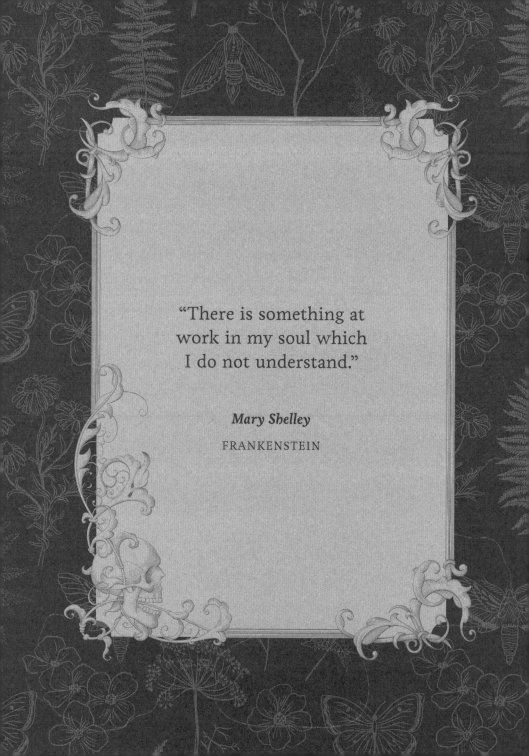

"There is something at
work in my soul which
I do not understand."

Mary Shelley

FRANKENSTEIN

THE SUN.

STRENGTH.

JUSTICE.

THE WORLD.

THE HIGH PRIESTESS

THE HIEROPHANT

THE FOOL.

DEATH.

THE HERMIT.

THE MAGICIAN.

JUDGEMENT.

THE TOWER.

THE DEVIL.

THE LOVERS.

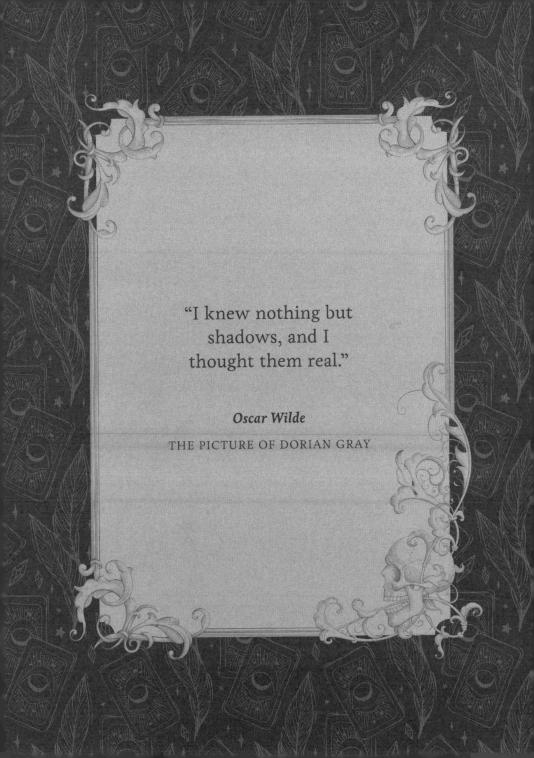

"I knew nothing but
shadows, and I
thought them real."

Oscar Wilde

THE PICTURE OF DORIAN GRAY

"Where there is
no imagination
there is no horror."

Sir Arthur Conan Doyle

A STUDY IN SCARLET

"A glimpse into the world
proves that horror is
nothing other than reality."

Alfred Hitchcock

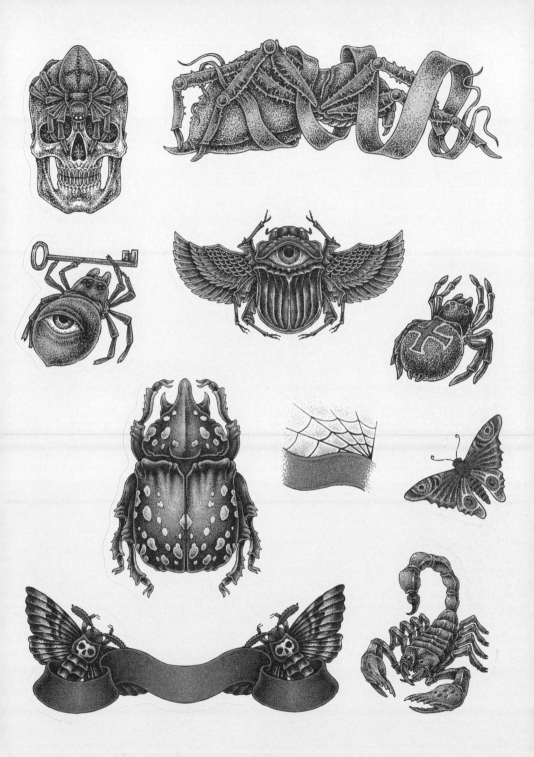

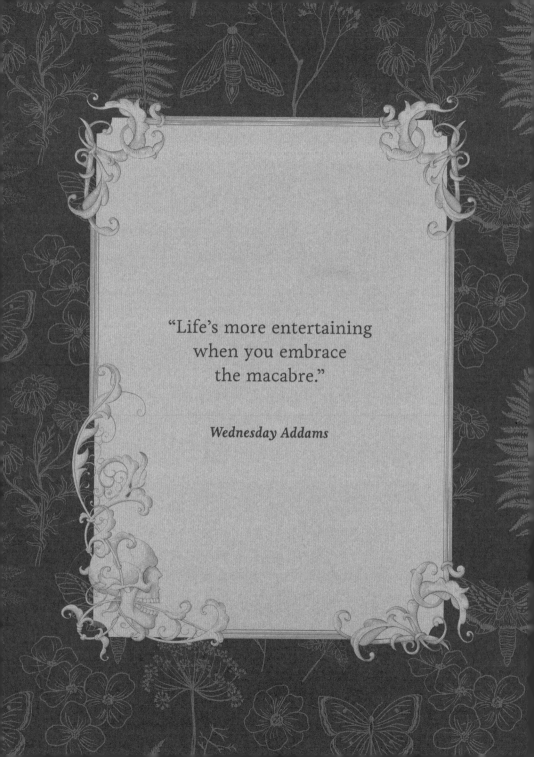

"Life's more entertaining
when you embrace
the macabre."

Wednesday Addams

"Thou art a poor soul,
saddled with a corpse."

Marcus Aurelius

"The emotions are sometimes so strong that I work without knowing it."

Vincent van Gogh

A Brief Tour of Tarot

No doubt you've come across tarot cards, in a variety of designs. You probably also know that tarot cards have been around for centuries. Over the past 600 years, people have consulted the cards for religious instruction, spiritual insight, self-knowledge, and divining the future. Think of tarot as a system of archetypes, a picture-book of the human condition, reflecting your state of mind and stage of life.

The basic methodology for tarot is simple. It draws on your innate ability to make connections, recognize yourself in the stories around you, and reinterpret signs with meaning. Your brain can bridge the gap between the archetypes presented on the cards and the events or elements of your own life that your intuition brings to the surface while you work with the cards. What matters is that you focus on yourself, the cards in front of you, and let the truth flow through you.

If you already have a tarot deck in hand, you can try a reading. On the next page is a short reference guide to what the different cards mean. After that are two popular ways of reading the cards.

0 THE FOOL *beginnings; risks*

I THE MAGICIAN *action; ambition; and manifesting*

II THE HIGH PRIESTESS *secrets; intuition; and learning*

III THE EMPRESS *creativity; resources; motherhood*

IV THE EMPEROR *order; power; and boundaries*

V THE HIEROPHANT *unity; marriage; and education*

VI THE LOVERS *love; decisions*

VII THE CHARIOT *progress; determination*

VIII STRENGTH *management; endurance*

IX THE HERMIT *analysis; solitude*

X THE WHEEL OF FORTUNE *luck; fate*

XI JUSTICE *decisions; balance; legal affairs*

XII THE HANGED MAN *waiting; sacrifice*

XIII DEATH *transformation; change; and new beginnings*

XIV TEMPERANCE *negotiation; moderation*

XV THE DEVIL *restriction; manipulation*

XVI THE TOWER *breakdown; illumination*

XVII THE STAR *hope;guidance*

XVIII THE MOON *crisis of faith; deep emotions*

XIX THE SUN *growth;recovery*

XX JUDGEMENT *the past; second chances*

XXI THE WORLD *success; completion*

CUPS

ACE *love; fertility; beginnings*
TWO *partnerships; relationships*
THREE *celebration; community*
FOUR *boredom; stasis*
FIVE *loss; sadness*
SIX *peace; a visitor*
SEVEN *confusion; possibilities*
EIGHT *departure; abandonment*
NINE *a wish come true; abundance*
TEN *happiness; family*
PAGE *fun; socializing*
KNIGHT *a dreamer; a proposal*
QUEEN *an intuitive woman; sensitivity*
KING *a warmhearted man; support*

PENTACLES

ACE *money; success; beginnings*
TWO *decisions; balance*
THREE *showing your talent; collaboration*
FOUR *stability; money management*
FIVE *financial loss; exclusion*
SIX *generosity; charity*
SEVEN *potential for success; perserverance*
EIGHT *money coming; skills*
NINE *material comforts; success*
TEN *inheritance; good business; marriage*
PAGE *an offer; management*
KNIGHT *a dependable man; trustworthy*
QUEEN *a generous woman; support*
KING *a prosperous man; security*

SWORDS

ACE *success; clarity*
TWO *stalemate; choice*
THREE *heartbreak; grief*
FOUR *rest; recharge*
FIVE *conflict; defeat*
SIX *leaving conflict behind; transition*
SEVEN *theft; deception*
EIGHT *restriction; feeling trapped*
NINE *anxiety; fears*
TEN *endings; suffering*
PAGE *gossip; contracts*
KNIGHT *battles; an opponent*
QUEEN *an independent woman; knowledge*
KING *a strong-willed man; divorce*

WANDS

ACE *news; male fertility; beginnings*
TWO *making plans; on the move*
THREE *travel; activity*
FOUR *a holiday; celebration*
FIVE *strong opinions; competition*
SIX *victory; success*
SEVEN *advocacy; standing strong*
EIGHT *news; swiftly moving*
NINE *strength; perserverance*
TEN *a burden; feeling overwhelmed*
PAGE *a message; enthusiasm*
KNIGHT *speed; an offer*
QUEEN *a creative woman; confidence*
KING *a creative man; motivational*

Past, Present, Future Card Reading

This easy spread is perfect for mini-readings. Shuffle the cards and cut the deck, then draw the top card and place it in slot one, the next card in slot two, and the last in slot three. Or fan the cards and choose three that speak to you, then lay them as shown. Each card represents the designated time (past, present, future). Reflect on the cards, their relationship to one another, and your interpretation.

Date: _____

Question asked: _____

_____

_____

_____

_____

_____

_____

❶	❷	❸
PAST	PRESENT	FUTURE
☐↑ ☐↓	☐↑ ☐↓	☐↑ ☐↓

Card drawn (note if upright ↑ or reversed ↓):

1. Past: _____

2. Present: _____

3. Future: _____

Keywords, themes, or symbols that come to mind: _____

_____

_____

Interpretation and reflection: _____

_____

_____

_____

The Celtic-Cross

The Celtic Cross is one of most popular tarot spreads because it answers a question or, if you don't have an immediate question, gives an overview of your life just now. Set your intention before you begin, asking your question as you shuffle. Shuffle and choose the cards and then lay them out as shown. If the tenth card is a court card—a Page, Knight, Queen, or King—then the outcome of the question is up to you.

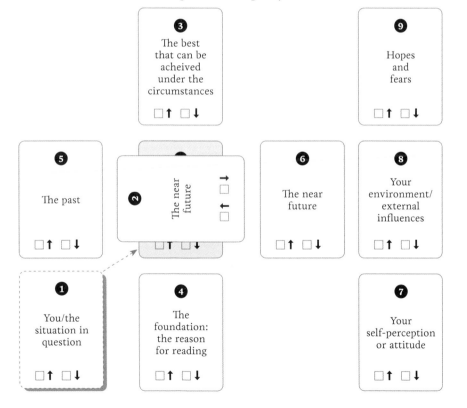

10 The outcome

3 The best that can be acheived under the circumstances □↑ □↓

9 Hopes and fears □↑ □↓

5 The past □↑ □↓

2 The near future → □ ← □ □↑ □↓

6 The near future □↑ □↓

8 Your environment/ external influences □↑ □↓

1 You/the situation in question □↑ □↓

4 The foundation: the reason for reading □↑ □↓

7 Your self-perception or attitude □↑ □↓

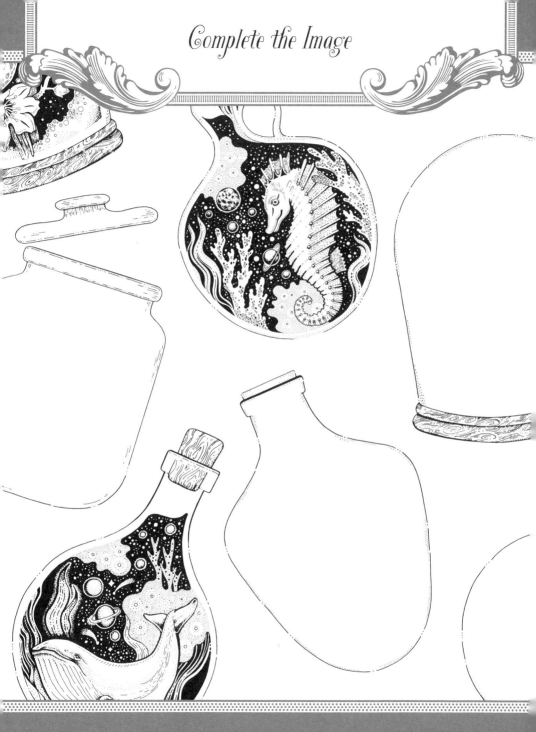

Color in the structure, then *decorate* with stickers.
See what you can *create!*

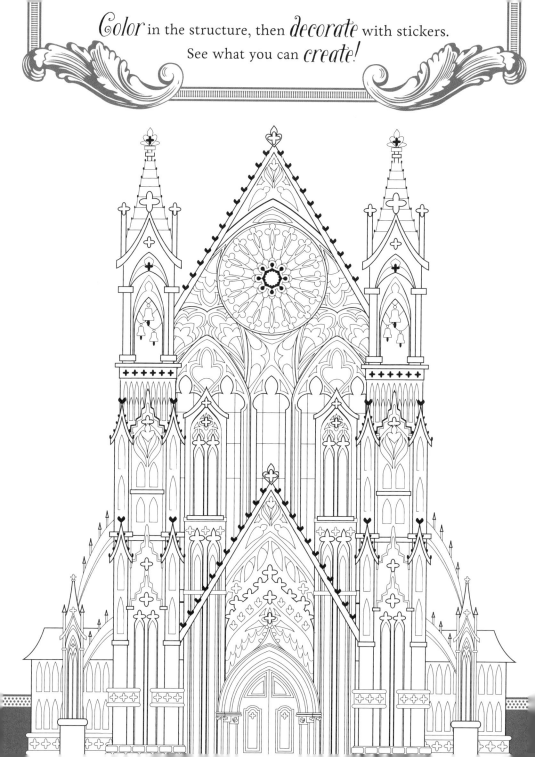

What's Your Odd & Curious Sign?

ARIES ram their way through life. They are driven, ambitious, optimistic, and brave. Crystals and herbs for Aries include bloodstone, carnelian, red jasper, cayenne, ginger, and yarrow.

TAURUS slowly pushes through obstacles with sheer determination. They are dedicated, hardworking, resourceful, and dependable. Crystals and herbs for Taurus include emerald, malachite, rose quartz, cardamom, rose, and sage.

GEMINI needs intellectual stimulation; they need to explore everything and talk to everyone. They are curious, intelligent, adaptable, and skilled communicators. Crystals and herbs for Gemini include citrine, howlite, tiger's eye, dill, lavender, and peppermint.

CANCERS naturally feel the emotions of others. It's why they need such a hard shell to protect their soft, sensitive souls. They are comforting, protective, sympathetic, and creative. Crystals and herbs for Cancer include moonstone, opal, selenite, aloe, chamomile, and lemon balm.

LEOS have a royal air around them that makes them worthy of a crown. They are charismatic, passionate, vibrant, and generous. Crystals and herbs for Leo include pyrite, ruby, sunstone, calendula, St. John's wort, and sunflower.

VIRGO represents belonging to oneself. They are capable, analytical, grounded, and helpful. Crystals and herbs for Virgo include amazonite, moss agate, peridot, cornflower, licorice root, and skullcap.

LIBRAS are all about balance, wanting to make life fair and peaceable for everyone. They are charming, artistic, harmonious, and romantic. Crystals and herbs for Libra include ametrine, pink tourmaline, sapphire, passionflower, rooibos, and violet.

SCORPIOS want to transform their lives for the highest good. They are quietly bold, capable, powerful, and intuitive. Crystals and herbs for Scorpio include labradorite, sodalite, yellow topaz, basil, coriander, and wormwood.

SAGITTARIUS is always on the move. They are independent, philosophical, friendly, and cheerful. Crystals and herbs for Sagittarius include blue topaz, green aventurine, turquoise, carnation, dandelion, and red clover.

CAPRICORN will not rest until they reach the top of whatever mountain they are trying to climb. They are ambitious, responsible, and purposeful. Crystals and herbs for Capricorn include garnet, smoky quartz, obsidian, rosemary, shepherd's purse, and thyme.

AQUARIUS seems to be a creature from another world, because they are so ahead of the crowd in every way. They are original, idealistic, curious, and innovative. Crystals and herbs for Aquarius include clear quartz, fluorite, hematite, cacao, fennel, and star anise.

PISCES energy flows all over the place. While they are quiet on the outside, they have a vivid inner life. They are imaginative, honest, and compassionate. Crystals and herbs for Pisces include amethyst, black tourmaline, calcite, lilac, mugwort, and witch hazel.

Encase Your Curious Finds in Resin Forever

Creating art with resin and found objects can be a great way to express yourself. (It's also easier than at-home taxidermy!) You can use dried flowers, seashells, beads, sequins, feathers, or dead bugs to create paperweights, jewelry, gifts, and other keepsakes. Here's how to do it.

What you'll need:

- Jewelry-grade acrylic resin or (if preserving insects) clear polyester casting resin
- Resin dye or powdered pigment (optional); do not use paint or food coloring
- Silicone molds (jewelry molds, if desired)
- Wooden stirring sticks (tongue depressors, crafting sticks, or chopsticks)
- Disposable plastic drinking cup
- Disposable gloves
- Toothpicks
- Tweezers
- Inserts (see Adding Inserts, page 112)
- Drop cloth or newspaper (for easy cleanup!)

What you'll do:

1. Prepare your workplace by laying down newspaper or other protective covering. Resin can be a messy craft! It is also recommended to wear protective gloves.

2. If using acrylic resin, mix an equal amount of resin base with the hardener. (For example, mix 5 mL of base and 5 mL of hardener in the mixing cup.) If using polyester resin, follow the instructions on your package, starting with the base and adding in the catalyst in the recommended amounts. Stir together using the stirring stick for 3 to 5 minutes to thoroughly combine, making sure to scrape the sides of the mixing cup to ensure all the resin is incorporated. Take your time measuring and stirring. Impatient mixing will add lots of tiny bubbles to the resin and may create a cloudy appearance to the finished piece.

3. Add resin dye, if using, and mix thoroughly. If you want to add glitter that is evenly spaced throughout your piece, mix it in at this time. If you want larger patches or streaks of glitter, you can try pouring small piles or lines of glitter directly onto the resin before (or after) you pour it into the mold. Let your resin mixture sit for 5 minutes before you begin pouring. This will allow the air bubbles to rise to the surface to pop.

4. While the resin mixture sits, rinse and dry the silicone mold to make sure it is free of dust.

5. Slowly pour the resin from the mixing cup into the resin mold. The resin is self-leveling but you can also use a toothpick to help it spread to each corner of the mold. Avoid overfilling the mold.

Marble Technique
Create one-of-a-kind pieces by swirling resin in your mold. To create this marble effect, stir small batches of two or more colors of resin. Use opaque pigmented dye for the boldest results. Pour the first color into one side of the mold then introduce a second and third color. Use a toothpick to gently swirl the colors into a marble-like pattern.

After resin has been poured into the mold, tiny air bubbles may rise to the surface. To remove them, you can use a toothpick or gently pass the flame from a lighter or a crafting heat gun approximately 1 inch (2.5 cm) above the surface of the resin. (DO NOT touch the resin with lighter or heat gun.) The heat will cause the bubbles to pop. If you do not pop the bubbles, they will become encased in the resin as it hardens (which may or may not be something you want to incorporate into your design).

6. The resin has a 30-minute work time before it begins to cure. Poke the surface with a toothpick to see if it's thick (but not gelatinous); you can also pop any air bubbles near the surface. Allow at least 24 hours cure time before removing your piece from the mold—3 to 4 days, if you can. (The surface will be tacky for a few days.)

7. When your piece is fully cured, pop it out of the silicon mold. Gently sand any rough edges, if needed.

Adding Inserts

Setting dried flowers, shells, beads, images printed on transparent film, or dead bugs (like crickets, wasps, flies, or spiders) inside clear resin can create fantastic and whimsical jewelry and other pieces of art. (But first, submerge any insects in ethanol or rubbing alcohol for at least 10 minutes to kill bacteria; when you're ready to use it, remove from the alcohol and allow to completely air dry, at least 30 minutes.) For best results, pour a thin layer (1/4 inch [0.64 cm]) of resin in the bottom of the mold and allow it to cure for 30 minutes. Then place your inserts into the mold (tweezers may be helpful for arranging small items). Wait 5 to 10 minutes before slowly pouring in another layer of resin to cover and follow directions from Step 6 on the previous page.

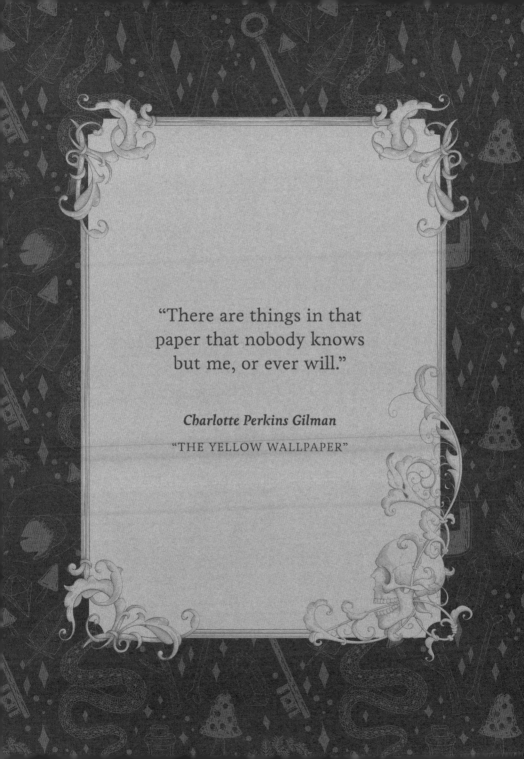

"There are things in that paper that nobody knows but me, or ever will."

Charlotte Perkins Gilman

"THE YELLOW WALLPAPER"

"*All* that we see or seem
Is but a dream within a dream."

Edgar Allan Poe

"A DREAM WITHIN A DREAM"

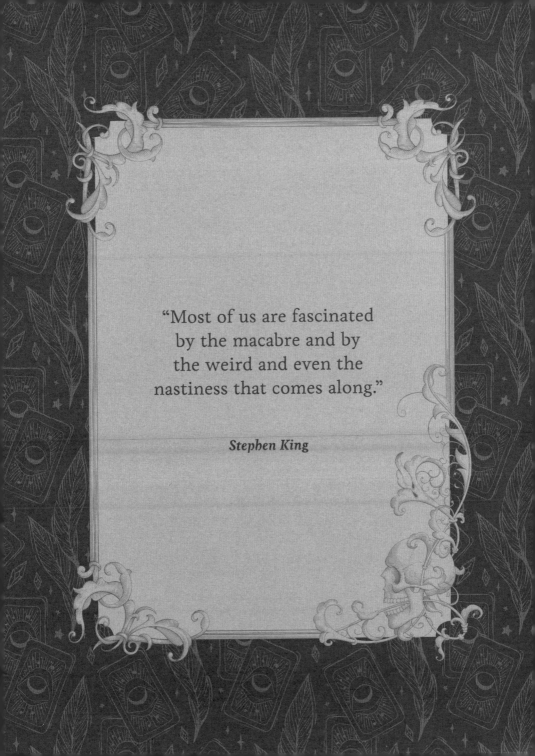

"Most of us are fascinated
by the macabre and by
the weird and even the
nastiness that comes along."

Stephen King

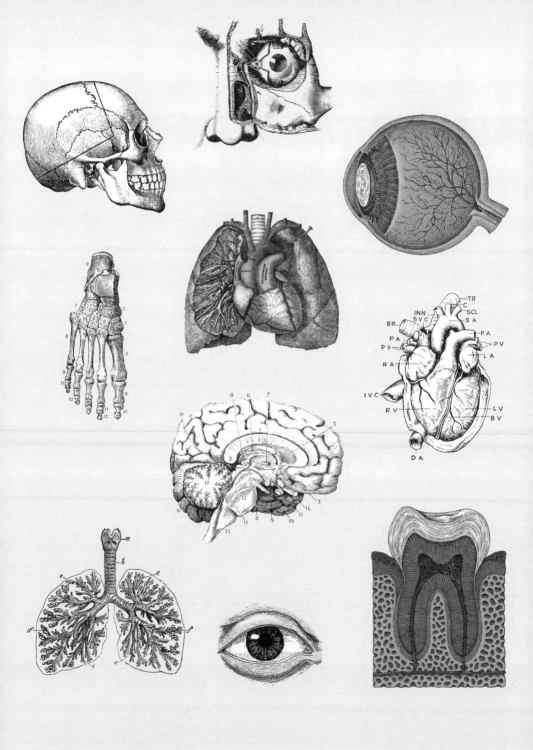

"Beware, for I am fearless
and therefore powerful."

Mary Shelley

FRANKENSTEIN

answers on page 170

Craft Your Own Lip Balm

Make like Cleopatra and put your artistic skills to another use by DIY-ing signature lip balms. Nothing is easier than melting together beeswax and natural oils.

Beeswax, produced as part of the honeycomb-building process, is the binder that holds the balm's ingredients together. It seals in moisture, kills germs, and conditions the skin—probably why it's been used to create art, make candles, protect food, and embalm mummies!

Use any base oil you prefer: olive, safflower, canola, corn, grapeseed, sunflower, almond, coconut, or avocado.

What you'll need:

- 1 tsp (5 mL) oil
- ½ tsp (2.5 mL) beeswax pastilles (found at craft stores or online)
- Measuring spoons
- Microwave
- 1-cup (225 mL) microwave-safe measure
- Wooden stir stick
- Add-ins (optional, see next page)
- Balm mold or tin (available online)

What you'll do:

Combine the oil and beeswax in the measuring cup. Microwave 30 seconds on high, then stir. If beeswax is not melted, heat in 10-second intervals until it is. Stir in any add-ins. Pour the mixture into your preferred mold or tin, wiping away any excess. Let harden for 25 minutes. Decorate your mold with stickers, if desired, and enjoy! (Discard balm after 2 months.)

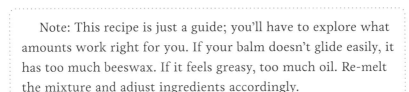

Note: This recipe is just a guide; you'll have to explore what amounts work right for you. If your balm doesn't glide easily, it has too much beeswax. If it feels greasy, too much oil. Re-melt the mixture and adjust ingredients accordingly.

Add-ins:

You don't need to do exactly as Cleopatra did—adding crushed cochineal carmine beetles to her beeswax balm—but you can mix in one or more of these ingredients:

- Candy coloring oils (found with candy-making supplies; start with the tiniest amount possible; do not use food coloring!)
- Candy flavoring oils (found with candy-making supplies; use only 1 or 2 drops)
- Chocolate chips (any flavor)
- Cocoa butter, grated
- Liquid glycerin
- Cosmetic-grade glitter (found in craft stores)
- Honey
- Lemon-flavored oil
- Chocolate-hazelnut spread
- Vanilla extract
- Sweet almond oil
- Lipstick shavings (for color)

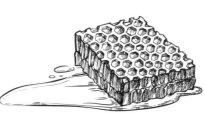

Sudoku

	2		4	8				6
6	9						8	5
8			9		1	3	7	
3		8	2			6		4
	6	9				2	5	7
2		5		4	7			
	8					5	2	3
						7		

solution on page 172

Trivia: Part II

1. Hanging in a cathedral in Ponte Nossa, Italy, is the earliest known mount (taxidermy) in existence, dating back to at least 1534. What is the animal on display?
A. monkey
B. crocodile
C. dodo bird
D. goat

2. What is the name of the moth that looks like it has a skull on its back?

3. Which species does NOT eat its partner after mating?
A. black widow
B. praying mantis
C. weevil
D. biting midge

4. True or False: The steampunk aesthetic takes its inspiration from the Victorian era.

5. Which country first used the plague doctor costume to protect doctors from their patients' illnesses?

6. What mushroom begins to devour itself once it's picked?

7. True or False: Early taxidermists stuffed mounts with wood chips and newspaper.

8. Which band does not fall under a Goth subgenre of music:
A. The Cure
B. Depeche Mode
C. Bauhaus
D. The Clash

9. Shrunken heads, also known as tsantsas, are real. What were the heads boiled in to shrink them?

10. What is the life stage of some insects where they transform between immature and mature forms?

answers on page 173

Sudoku

		3		7	9	6		
				5		9	1	
	9	8	2		4		5	7
7		1				5		9
				2	1		7	
	2		7	9	5		6	3
4		6						5
			5				9	
9				3			8	

solution on page 174

Caption This!

What Is Your *Gothic Name?*

Match the first letter of your first or last name with the first list of names. Then match the day you were born with the second list of names. Now you have your Gothic name—perhaps it can be your pen name on a modern-day gothic novel!

Sir/Madame/Doctor:

_____

A	Evalina	J	Vincent	S	Melodie
B	Griffin	K	Lycia	T	Erastus
C	Lydia	L	Remus	U	Ruby
D	Alistair	M	Poppy	V	Salazar
E	Marissa	N	Jasper	W	Arachne
F	Gregor	O	Ember	X	Cassius
G	Opal	P	Zachariah	Y	Morgana
H	Xanthos	Q	Angelique	Z	Solomon
I	Infinity	R	Morpheus		

1	Mortella	12	Blackwood	23	Coffin
2	Crowley	13	Widdowes	24	Mort
3	LaRue	14	Deathridge	25	Redwine
4	Radcliffe	15	Deadmond	26	Chillingwood
5	Wolfstone	16	Ravendale	27	Coldbridge
6	Winterrose	17	Bonesmith	28	Sorrows
7	Ripley	18	Pyre	29	Barker
8	Chillingsworth	19	Storm	30	Moan
9	Fury	20	Toothman	31	LeStrange
10	Windward	21	Featherby		
11	Gorey	22	Ravenhorst		

Have Fun with *Shadow Puppets!*

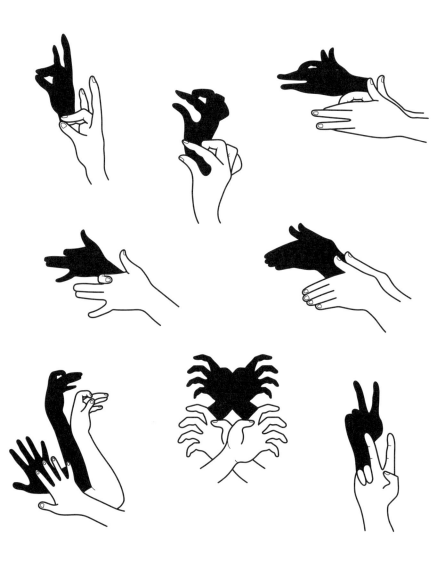

solution on page 175

solution on page 176

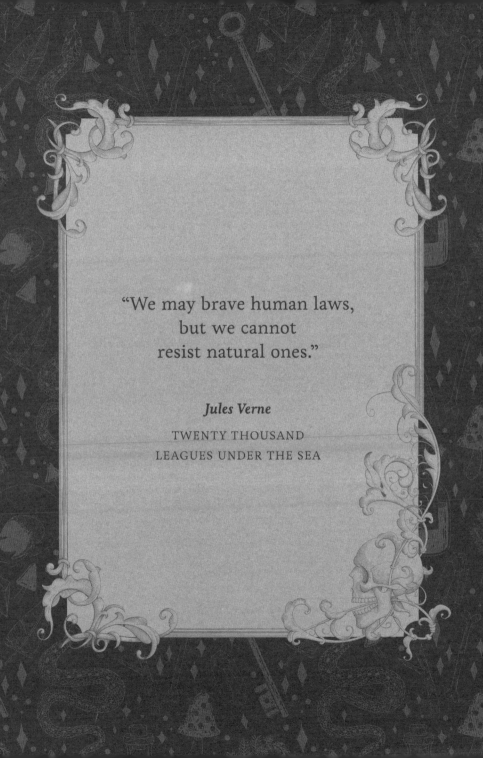

"We may brave human laws,
but we cannot
resist natural ones."

Jules Verne

TWENTY THOUSAND
LEAGUES UNDER THE SEA

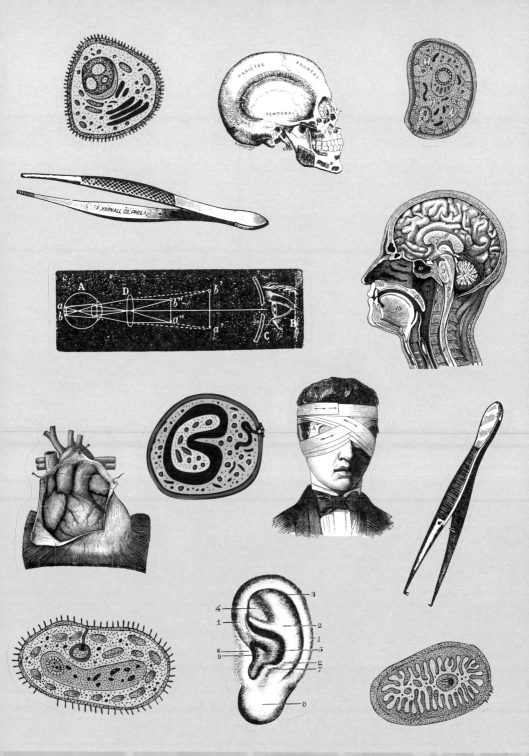

"I want you to believe...
To believe in things
that you cannot."

Bram Stoker

DRACULA

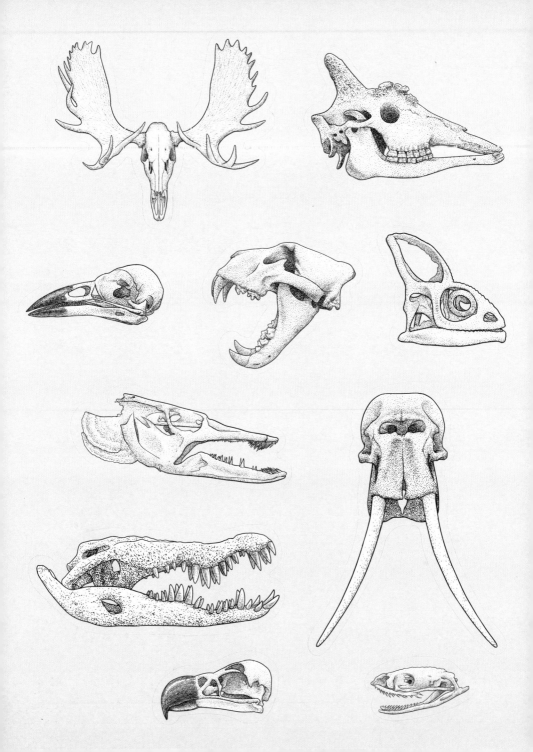

"Unfathomable to mere mortals is the lore of fiends."

Nathaniel Hawthorne

"YOUNG GOODMAN BROWN"

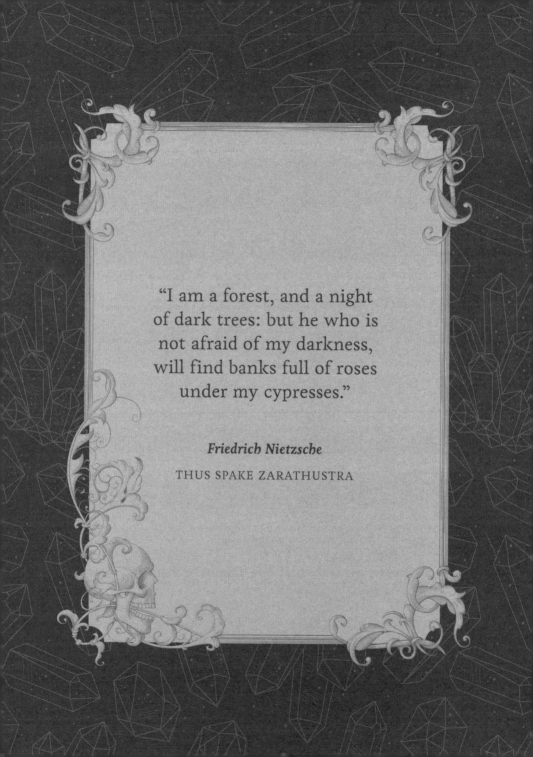

"I am a forest, and a night
of dark trees: but he who is
not afraid of my darkness,
will find banks full of roses
under my cypresses."

Friedrich Nietzsche

THUS SPAKE ZARATHUSTRA

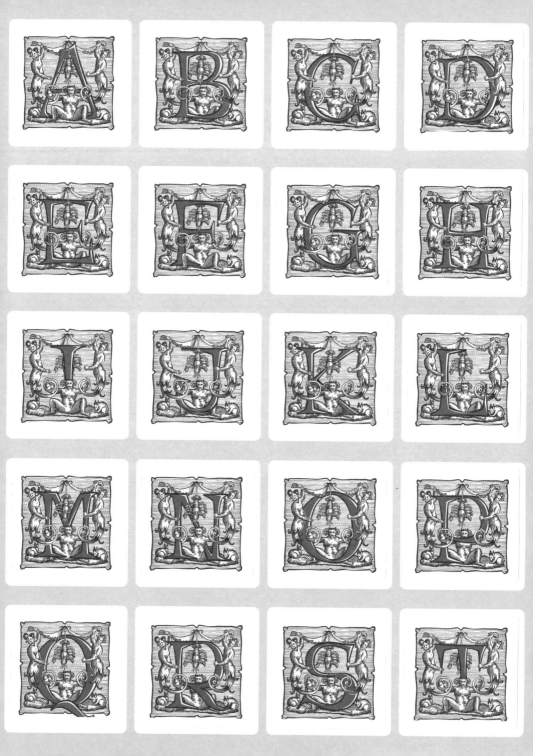

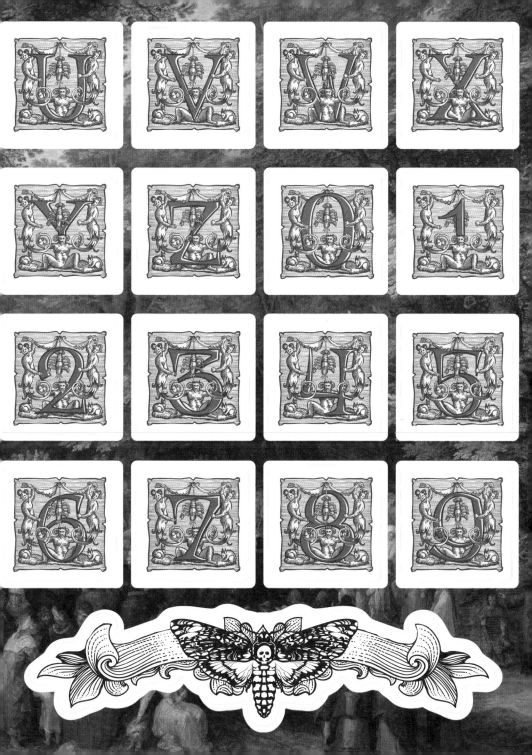

*maze on
page 8*

*maze on
page 9*

*maze on
page 10*

*maze on
page 11*

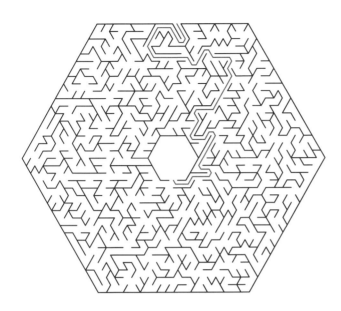

*maze on
page 12*

*maze on
page 13*

maze on pagc 14

maze on page 15

maze on page 16

Trivia: Part I

(answer key)

1. What is considered the first gothic novel?

Though many might think of Mary Shelley's Frankenstein *(1818), it was* The Castle of Otranto *by Horace Walpole (1764) that gets the credit.*

2. Who wrote *The Turn of the Screw*?

Henry James

3. What was special about Dorian Gray's picture?

The picture ages while Dorian remains young.

4. True or False: Dr. Jekyll turned into Mr. Hyde when he drank wine.

False. Dr. Jekyll developed a potion; though later, Mr. Hyde was able to emerge without it.

5. What character is this?

Jane Eyre

6. True or False: Jane Austen wrote a parody of a gothic novel.

True. Austen's Northanger Abbey was a parody or satire of gothic novels.

7. Though Edgar Allen Poe is buried in Baltimore, in which city is his National Historic Site?

Philadelphia

8. What is the name of the English estate purchased by Dracula?

Carfax (Bram Stoker did not write "Carfax Abbey" in the book.)

9. *The Addams Family* characters started as a cartoon in which magazine?

The New Yorker

10. Which building in Washington, D.C., has a Darth Vader grotesque (gargoyle)?

Washington National Cathedral

trivia on page 48

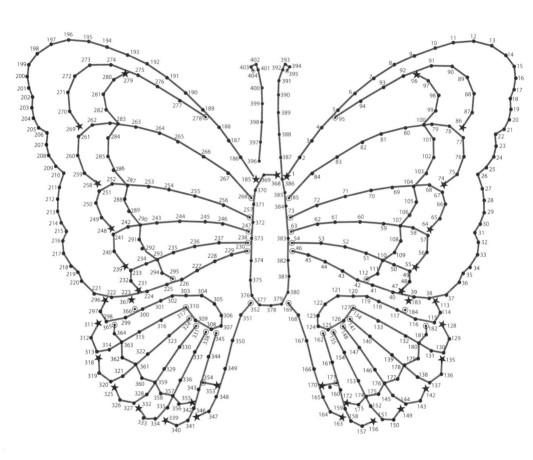

puzzle on page 44

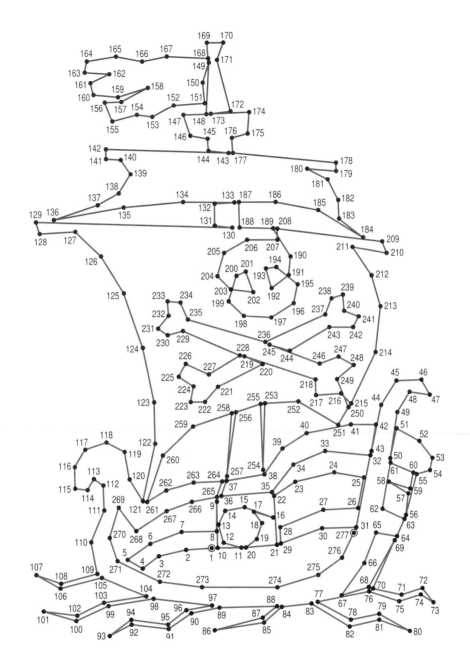

puzzle on page 45

puzzle on page 46

puzzle on page 47

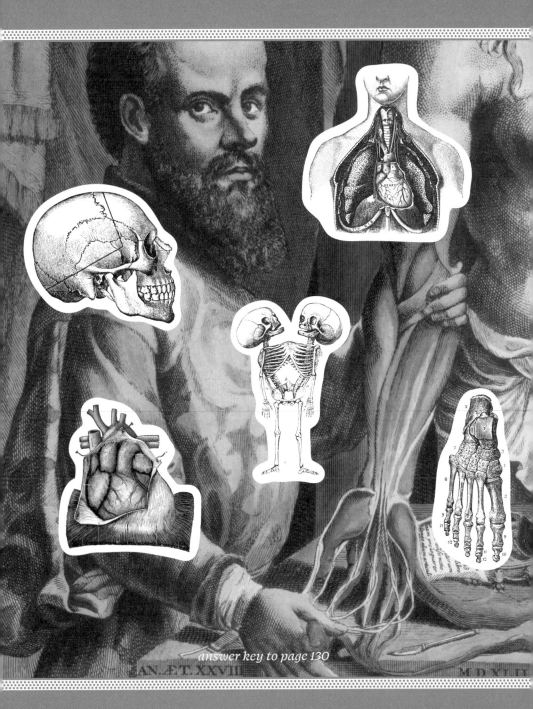

answer key to page 130

AN. ÆT. XXVII

M D XLII

Sudoku
(answer key)

7	2	3	4	8	5	1	9	6
6	9	1	3	7	2	4	8	5
8	5	4	9	6	1	3	7	2
3	7	8	2	5	9	6	1	4
4	6	9	1	3	8	2	5	7
2	1	5	6	4	7	9	3	8
9	4	7	5	2	3	8	6	1
1	8	6	7	9	4	5	2	3
5	3	2	8	1	6	7	4	9

puzzle on page 134

Trivia: Part II
(answer key)

1. Hanging in a cathedral in Ponte Nossa, Italy, is the earliest known mount (taxidermy) in existence, dating back to at least 1534. What is the animal on display?
A. monkey
B. crocodile
C. dodo bird
D. goat

2. What is the name of the moth that looks like it has a skull on its back?

Death's-head hawkmoth

3. Which species does NOT eat its partner after mating?
A. black widow
B. praying mantis
C. weevil
D. biting midge

4. True or False: The steampunk aesthetic takes its inspiration from the Victorian era.

True

5. Which country first used the plague doctor costume to protect doctors from their patients' illnesses?

The plague costume was developed by physician Charles de Lorme in France around 1619.

6. What mushroom begins to devour itself once it's picked?

Shaggy ink caps, or shaggy manes, use auto-digestion that will turn them into black goo within 24 hours of being picked.

7. True or False: Early taxidermists stuffed mounts with wood chips and newspaper.

False. They used sawdust and rags.

8. Which band does not fall under a Goth subgenre of music:
A. The Cure
B. Depeche Mode
C. Bauhaus
D. The Clash

9. Shrunken heads, also known as tsantsas, are real. What were the heads boiled in to shrink them?

Water

10. What is the life stage of some insects where they transform between immature and mature forms?

Pupa

trivia on page 135

Sudoku

(answer key)

2	5	3	1	7	9	6	4	8
6	4	7	8	5	3	9	1	2
1	9	8	2	6	4	3	5	7
7	6	1	3	4	8	5	2	9
5	3	9	6	2	1	8	7	4
8	2	4	7	9	5	1	6	3
4	8	6	9	1	7	2	3	5
3	7	2	5	8	6	4	9	1
9	1	5	4	3	2	7	8	6

puzzle on page 136

maze on page 142

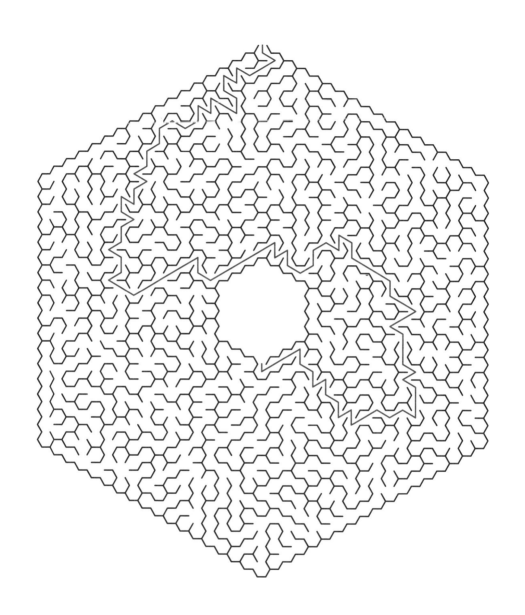

maze on page 143

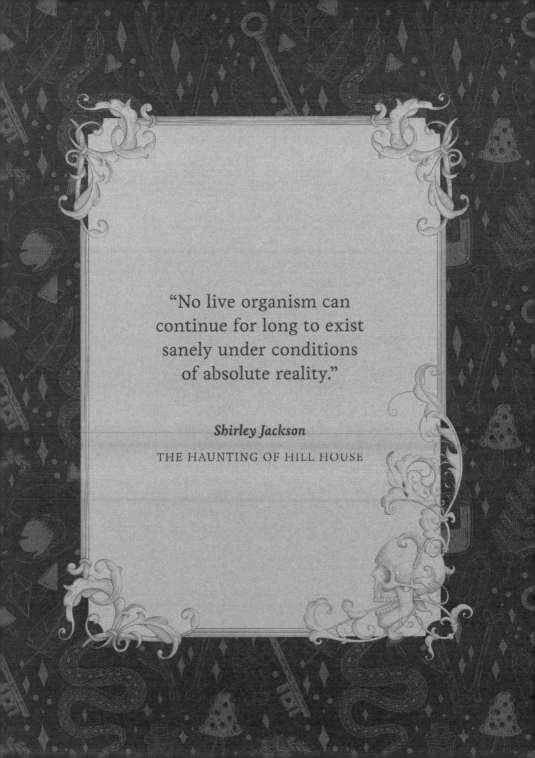

"No live organism can
continue for long to exist
sanely under conditions
of absolute reality."

Shirley Jackson

THE HAUNTING OF HILL HOUSE

"Creativity
takes courage."

Henri Matisse

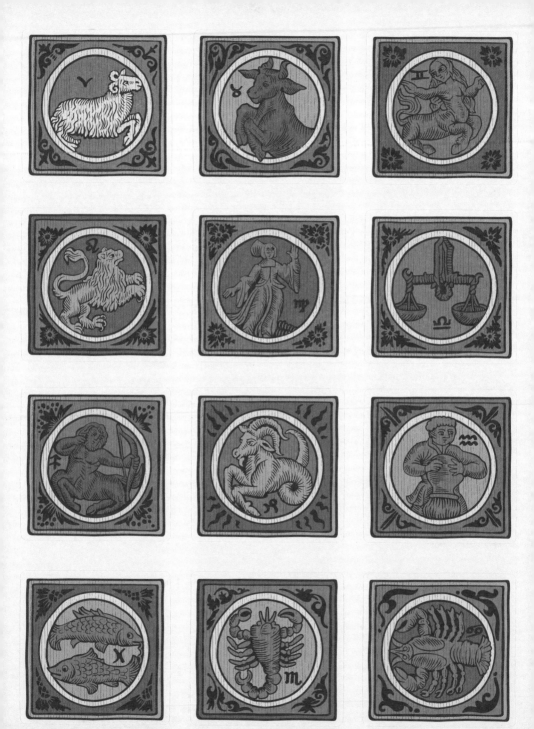

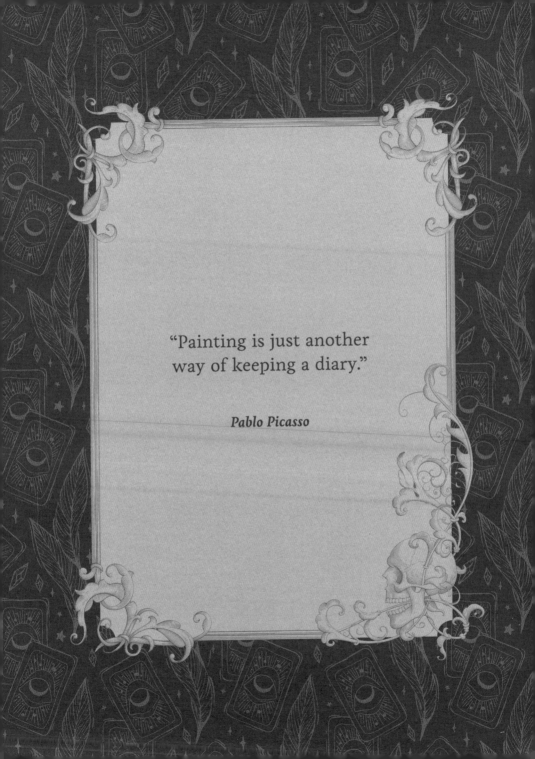

"Painting is just another
way of keeping a diary."

Pablo Picasso

"Never to suffer would
have been never to
have been blessed."

Edgar Allan Poe